Careers in Construction

Electrician

Jeri Freedman

Cavendish
Square
New York

Published in 2016 by Cavendish Square Publishing, LLC
243 5th Avenue, Suite 136, New York, NY 10016

First Edition

Website: cavendishsq.com

This publication represents the opinions and views of the author based on his or her personal experience, knowledge, and research. The information in this book serves as a general guide only. The author and publisher have used their best efforts in preparing this book and disclaim liability rising directly or indirectly from the use and application of this book.

CPSIA Compliance Information: Batch #CW16CSQ

All websites were available and accurate when this book was sent to press.

Cataloging-in-Publication Data

Freedman, Jeri.
Electrician / by Jeri Freedman.
p. cm. — (Careers in construction)
Includes index.
ISBN 978-1-5026-0980-9 (hardcover) ISBN 978-1-5026-0981-6 (ebook)
1. Electrical engineering — Vocational guidance — Juvenile literature.
2. Electricians — Juvenile literature. I. Freedman, Jeri. II. Title.
TK159.F74 2016
621.319'24'023—d23

Editorial Director: David McNamara
Editors: Andrew Coddington and Kelly Spence
Copy Editor: Rebecca Rohan
Art Director: Jeffrey Talbot
Designer: Alan Sliwinski
Senior Production Manager: Jennifer Ryder-Talbot
Production Editor: Renni Johnson
Photo Research: J8 Media

The photographs in this book are used by permission and through the courtesy of: K. Miri Photography/ Shutterstock.com, cover; nahariyani/Shutterstock.com, cover and used throughout the book; Ant Clausen/ Shutterstock.com, 4; DreamPictures/Shannon Faulk/Getty Images, 8; Shaiith/Shutterstock.com, 10; Everett Historical/Shutterstock.com, 14; IVV79/iStockphoto.com, 16; BlueRingMedia/Shutterstock.com, 18; Ulrich Baumgarten/Getty Images, 30; Cultura/Getty Images, 38; Nahariyani/Shutterstock.com, 41; Lisa F. Young/Shutterstock.com, 46; U.S. Navy/Photographer's Mate 3rd Class John E. Woods/File:US Navy 040422-N-9849W-036 Sailors work together to repair a damaged engine on an SH-3 Sea King helicopter aboard USS Coronado (AGF 11).jpg, 49; Monty Rakusen/Getty Images, 55; Atomazul/Shutterstock.com, 56; Dmitry Kalinovsky/Shutterstock.com, 58, 65, 68; Pixelsnap/Shutterstock.com, 60; Purdue9394/Shutterstock. com, 71; Stephen Rudolph/Shutterstock.com, 73; Cvisphoto/iStock.com, 80; KarenMower/iStockphoto. com, 95; s-c-s/iStockphoto.com, 97; Energy.gov/File:Installing Solar Panels (7336033672).jpg, 99; nadla/ iStockphoto.com, 101; bikeriderlondon/Shutterstock.com, 103.

Printed in the United States of America

Table of Contents

Working as an electrician can be a highly satisfying career because you play a crucial role in the creation of new buildings.

Introduction

Schools, houses, hospitals, shopping malls, airports, and every other building we enter in the course of the day were built by members of the construction industry. Every one of these buildings includes features installed by electricians. The lights; security systems; heating, cooling, and ventilation systems (HVAC); video screens and sound systems; and computer networks and telecommunications are all functioning because of electricians. The electrical trade has been critical to the construction of buildings since electricity entered common use at the end of the nineteenth century. In today's electronically connected world, however, electricians play a bigger role than ever before.

The primary role of an electrician is to install the necessary electrical **infrastructure** (wiring and devices) in a building to keep electrical current flowing in a safe and reliable manner to switches, outlets, fixtures, appliances, and equipment. The electrician may perform other activities, depending on the type of construction, the nature of the industry in which he or she is employed, and his or her level of experience. An electrician may be hired by a **general contractor** to work as a **subcontractor** on new construction, or hired directly by homeowners or business owners.

When you become an electrician, you learn a trade. Learning a trade means you become an expert in a particular field, and that expertise allows you to find work throughout your life. Knowing a trade allows you the flexibility to apply your skills in a variety of ways. Working in a construction trade can give you the option of working on the projects that you choose to undertake. It also gives you the option of choosing the security of working for someone else when you are starting out, as well as the option of being independent later in your career.

Why might you be interested in a career as an electrician? Even though the economy has recovered to a degree since the crash of 2008, it is still difficult for many people to get jobs. This is especially true for students who are looking for work right out of high school. Learning a trade gives you the ability to be self-sufficient and self-reliant. It offers you a number of career paths with increasing levels of responsibilities. A career in the electrical field can provide you with lifetime job security and a steady income. There are good job opportunities for electricians, and their income increases over time as they gain more skills. Electricians have the opportunity to work in a variety of environments and to learn specialties that interest them and provide higher earnings.

As homes and businesses incorporate more electric and electronic devices and systems, the demand for electricians will continue to grow. The development of new technologies for consumers, businesses, and factories will keep the job interesting in the future and open up new opportunities for experienced electricians.

Master electricians have the choice of many types of companies in which to work. They may work for a large or small **contractor,** for an electrical services company, or for themselves. They may specialize in residential construction or in commercial or industrial electrical applications. They may work on single-family homes, stores and restaurants, or vast complexes of buildings. Some electricians even choose to work overseas, which allows them to travel and experience other parts of the world. Being an electrician can offer you the satisfaction of contributing to the creation of facilities used by families, small business owners, and the community at large. Because electricians work collaboratively with other contractors, they are able to develop professional relationships with others in the industry.

There is more construction work during good economic times, and there may be more work at certain times of the year, in some parts of the country. However,

Electricians work in many different environments, which provide an interesting and challenging career.

electricians are needed in both good and bad economic times. The electrical systems in existing buildings, the power-generating industry, and industrial and commercial facilities need to be repaired, upgraded, and maintained under all conditions. Being an electrician always involves the challenge of problem solving.

Becoming an electrician requires a commitment to learning the required skills. However, it does not require going into college directly from high school. Most electricians enter apprentice programs that allow them to start earning a wage and learn the trade while they work. Unlike the classroom education students receive when studying for a college degree, the training to become an electrician is focused directly on the practical skills needed for a career. That said, taking on a job as an apprentice does not mean that you don't have to study. Electricians study course material and continue to learn skills on the job throughout their careers. Being an electrician requires you to have knowledge of math and the technology of electrical components. This means you have to study in classes or online, in addition to working. This is an excellent field for those who can apply themselves independently to learning after putting in a day's work. Working as an electrician also requires you to pay attention to details, for your safety and that of others.

It takes specific calculations and equipment to generate, produce, and measure an electric current.

CHAPTER 1

The Electrical Industry

lectrical phenomena have been observed since ancient times. As far back as 2750 BCE, Egyptian texts described fish that would give off a shock if touched. Electrical fish were also described in ancient Roman, Greek, and Arabian texts. The ancient Greeks observed the effects of lightning and noted that the poles of magnetic material would attract or repel each other. Thales of Miletus noted that rubbing amber with wool or fur would cause it to attract lightweight objects such as leaves, which we now know results from static electricity. However, the Greeks did not investigate the causes of these phenomena. The earliest recorded instance of an understanding of the electrical force that affected multiple objects was the Arabs' use of the word for lightning, *raad*, to describe the electric ray fish.

It was not until the seventeenth century that scientists began to investigate the principles of electricity. William Gilbert, an English physician and scientist, was the first to undertake a systematic study of the relationship between electricity and magnetism. In 1600, he published the book *De Magnete, Magneticisque Corporibus, et de Magno Magnete Tellure* (*On the Magnet and Magnetic Bodies, and on the Great Magnet the Earth*). He is considered the father of electrical engineering. In 1646, Sir Thomas Browne coined the word electricity, based on Gilbert's use of the term electron to describe materials that had the property of attracting other materials "like amber" (*elektron* is the Greek word for amber). In the eighteenth century, Benjamin Franklin studied electricity. Among his explorations was his famous kite experiment of 1752. He is said to have attached a metal key to a damp kite string before a thunderstorm. The series of sparks jumping down the string to the back of his hand confirmed his belief that lightning was an electrical phenomenon. In 1780, Italian scientist Luigi Galvani proved that a combination of two metals could be used to conduct electricity. In 1800, Alessandro Volta built on Galvani's work and created the first battery, consisting of alternating layers of zinc and copper. The electrical measure called the volt is named after him.

It was in the nineteenth century that electrical engineers began to devise the means of using electricity for residential and industrial needs. Michael Faraday created the first electric motor in 1821. Subsequently, he discovered that electricity could be made to flow through a wire, and he went on to make many other important discoveries in the field. German physicist George Ohm established the principles of the electrical **circuit** in 1827. In 1873, the Scottish scientist James Clerk Maxwell published the *Treatise on Electricity and Magnetism*, in which he demonstrated that electricity and magnetism are the result of one electromagnetic force.

The early nineteenth-century experiments in electricity laid the foundation for the practical use of electricity in the latter half of the nineteenth century. Alexander Graham Bell, experimenting with the use of electricity to create hearing devices, invented the telephone, which he patented in 1876. Throughout the late nineteenth and early twentieth centuries, Thomas Edison invented numerous electrical devices, including the phonograph and the lightbulb. However, his most important contribution to the history of construction was the development of a means of commercially generating electrical power and the first public electric utility, the Edison Illuminating Company, in 1880. In 1882, he began generating electrical power to Manhattan and London.

In 1887, Nikola Tesla, a Hungarian engineer living in the United States, designed an **alternating current** motor, which generated electricity that could be transmitted at a high **voltage** over long distances. Using Tesla's invention, George Westinghouse began generating electric power from his firm, Westinghouse Electric. The era of electrification had begun in earnest.

Alternating current generators like this one were used in early Westinghouse power plants to create electricity.

Principles of Electrification

Electricity is the process by which energy is generated when charged particles move from one place to another. What is a charged particle? The smallest unit of matter is the atom. Everything is made up of atoms. The central area of an atom is the nucleus, and it contains tiny particles called protons and neutrons. Neutrons have a neutral electrical charge; protons have a positive electrical charge. Electrons are negatively charged particles. They circle around the outside of the atom. Positively charged particles and negatively charged particles are attracted to each other. This fact can be used to make the particles move from one place to another, such as from one end of a wire to the other. When charged particles move from one location to another, they generate electrical current. This current can be used to power devices. Examples of electricity generated by moving particles include lightning, which results when electrons move from a cloud to the ground, and static electricity, which occurs when electrons jump from an object to a person—such as you, when you touch the object.

When electrons circle, or orbit, the nucleus of an atom, they create an electric field. Because the electrons move in different directions, the electrons in the atoms that make up most objects spin in different directions, and the effects

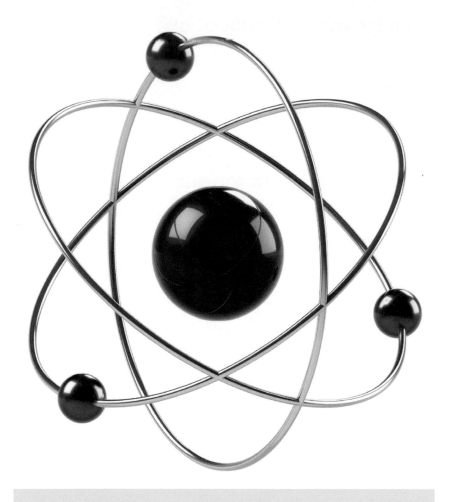

This illustration of an atom shows the electrons (blue) orbiting the nucleus (red).

of their magnetic fields cancel each other out. In magnets, however, the atoms are arranged so that the electrons all spin in the same direction. That is why a magnet has a north pole, or end, and a south pole. If you touch the opposite poles of two magnets together, they will attract each other and stick together. If you try to touch the same poles of two magnets together, they will repel each other.

If magnets are moved over a material with loosely held electrons, like copper, the magnetic field of the magnet will pull or push the electrons, causing them to move. This is how electric current is generated. Metals like copper are used in electric wires because the electrons in the copper atoms are easy to move. A magnet is used to move the electrons along the wire. This current is a form of energy and can be used to power equipment or devices.

In order to flow, electricity must have a closed (circular) path. This path is called a circuit, which is a Latin word meaning "it has circled." If the path is broken, the electricity cannot flow. This is the basic principle that electricians use for powering electrical equipment and electronic devices. For example, when a light is off, there is a gap in the circuit. When you flip the switch, it closes the circuit and electricity flows into the lightbulb then out the wire on the other side, causing the bulb to glow. The same is true when you turn on a computer. When it is off, the circuit is open. When you turn it on, the circuit is closed, and electricity flows down the wire to the components that power the computer and out another wire.

Electricity used in constructed buildings is produced by converting another form of energy into electricity by means of a generator. Generators are pieces of equipment

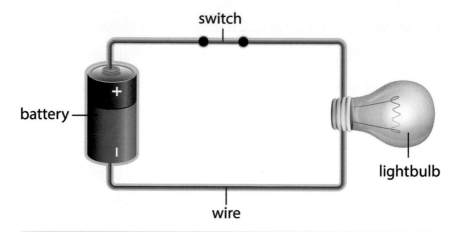

This simple circuit illustrates how electric current travels from the positive pole of a battery through the wire to an electrical device and back to the negative pole of the battery.

that use large coils of wire and an electromagnetic field (a magnet-like field produced by electricity) to convert another source of energy to electricity. Power plants use very large generators. Homeowners may have small generators to keep power going in case of emergency.

The energy that is used to produce electrical current can come from many sources. Among these are heat energy from burning coal, burning oil, or boiling water (steam); kinetic (motion-based) energy from moving water or wind; and light-based energy from the sun. Electricians must know how to create circuits and design a building to use electricity generated from particular sources.

What an Electrician Does

Electricians install and fix devices and wires that transmit electricity. They make it possible for people to use lights, appliances, and entertainment systems. They make it possible for businesses and factories to run equipment. Among the devices electricians install are light switches and light fixtures, ventilation fans, power outlets, **hardwired** smoke detectors, heating and cooling thermostats, and many other devices. There are many types of electricians. Most of them work in the residential field.

Residential electricians put wiring and electrical devices in homes. They might work on single-family or multi-family homes as well as apartments and condominiums. Sometimes residential electricians install wiring in new construction before the walls are closed up. They also update wiring and install new devices and equipment in finished homes. They might install wiring and devices for audio, video, computers, security systems, and air conditioning.

Commercial electricians install electric wires and devices in businesses, stores, office buildings, and other nonresidential buildings such as churches and schools. Whereas residential electricians often provide wiring for devices used in homes, such as appliances, commercial electricians often provide electrical connections for pumps, motors, and specialized equipment such as commercial stoves and freezers, pizza ovens, and other equipment used in shops and restaurants. In the case of office buildings, they perform the electrical part of the installation of commercial heating, air conditioning, and security systems, which function throughout the entire building.

Industrial electricians work on very large facilities, such as factories, airports, hospitals, sports arenas, and train stations. In addition to the kinds of systems installed in commercial enterprises, they install systems to run escalators, moving walkways, lighted announcement boards, ticketing machines, automated production lines, and fire alarms, among other applications.

What It Takes to Be an Electrician

Electricians must have certain skills to succeed in the industry. Some skills are practical. Electricians must have good manual dexterity—skill and ease in using their hands—and be good at taking things apart and putting them back together. Electricians spend a lot of time assembling and connecting things. They must be adept at monitoring equipment and testing equipment with technical devices. They must have an understanding of the principles of electricity so that they can interpret the significance of the readings they see on the screens of testing devices. They must know the safety procedures required to work around electrical devices to protect themselves and other people in the area where they are working. Electricians who work on large projects and facilities must have a strong understanding of mathematics so that they can correctly perform the calculations necessary to design a large system with many complex components.

Intellectual and interpersonal skills are also important. Electricians must be able to think logically and plan systematically. They must be able to map out each phase of a project and all the steps within each phase. Such planning is the key to a successful project. They must be able to accurately calculate the quantity and costs of the materials needed, and the number of hours it will take to complete the project. Miscalculations in these areas can result in project delays and/or loss of money for the electrician or the company he or she works for. Logical thinking also plays a role in troubleshooting. Electricians must be able to identify the source of a problem by systematically testing and eliminating possible causes until the correct one is identified.

Communication skills are very important. Electricians must be able to communicate clearly and positively with potential customers and other contractors. They must be able to convince potential clients that they can provide the services the customer needs. They must be able to explain problems to customers in a manner that is calm and pleasant, even if the customer is upset.

Commercial and industrial projects often involve many different types of contractors, such as carpenters, plumbers, landscapers, masons, and others. Very large projects usually employ multiple electricians because of the vast amount of work required. An electrician must be able to coordinate his or her work with that of other contractors and other electricians on such a project. Often on a construction project, one contractor cannot complete his or her work until another contractor finishes or installs necessary components. An electrical contractor must be able to work out an appropriate schedule that allows other contractors to get their work done in a timely fashion and the project to be finished on time. He or she must remain on good terms with other contractors during this project, because contractors often recommend professionals they've worked with for other projects, if they respect them. For the same reason, reliability is an important characteristic. Reliability means being where you say you will be when you are supposed to be there.

Electricians sometimes have to work outside, so they must be able to tolerate cold, heat, and possibly bad weather. Electricians who work primarily on residences

TOOLS OF THE TRADE

Electricians use hand, power, and electric tools in their work. For hand tools, they use **insulated** screwdrivers and nut drivers. The insulation helps protect them from shocks that might result from the metal tools or metal components coming in contact with wires. They also use a variety of pliers, including needle-nose and bent-nose pliers. They use wire strippers and cutters to remove insulation from wiring, so they can access the wires to make connections and hook up outlets, switches, and other devices.

Industrial and commercial electricians use machines called "pipe benders," which bend and cut pipe to prepare the **conduit** through which wiring runs. On large construction jobs, they may use an automatic wire feeder, which feeds wires into multiple pipes simultaneously. This can speed up the process of wiring a building and reduce the amount of labor required by the electrician. Electricians use electronic devices to test power lines in all types of electrical work. The most common test devices include circuit and voltage testers. Electricians carry hand and testing tools in either a tool belt or a toolbox when on the job.

and small businesses will usually work for a short period of time on a project, ranging from a few hours to a few weeks. However, on very large industrial projects, electricians will usually work for months or as long as a year.

Where Do Electricians Work?

Sometimes electricians work on homes or buildings while they are being constructed. In this case, they work in two phases. First, they install wiring during the rough phase of construction. At this point, the walls are still open. Then other contractors finish the walls, and the electrician returns to install outlets, light switches, and other devices in the surface of the walls. When electricians do work in the rough stage of construction, the building may be unfinished and open to the weather, so the working conditions may be hot or cold. Working in a building under construction requires great care. There are likely to be construction materials, tools, and equipment in the house as well as sharp or dangerous construction debris.

Sometimes electricians work in finished buildings. They may be called in to install additional outlets, install special connections for high-power items such as air conditioners, or hook up new equipment, such as a new security system. In this case, residential electricians may have to work in tight spaces, sometimes in cellars or attics crowded with many items. Electricians working in finished buildings must be able to do their work in a way that causes minimal damage to walls and other items in the vicinity.

Electricians working on commercial construction, such as a hospital, a school, or another large facility, work on sites that are often filled with large construction vehicles and equipment. They may prepare electrical components outside and then bring them into the building for installation. In multistory apartment and commercial buildings, electricians may have to work high above the ground to install wiring and components in the upper stories during the rough stage of construction. Residential electricians working in private homes usually work from 8 a.m. to 5 or 6 p.m., although they may work a bit later if they are on a job they can finish up that day. Electricians working on large construction projects—such as office buildings, apartment complexes, airports, schools, and hospitals—may have to work longer hours because these buildings often must be completed by a set deadline. In some cases, the general contractor may have to pay a fee to the client if the building is not done on time. Therefore, the electricians on the project may have to work well after dark, using large construction lights to see.

Many electricians work as independent contractors, which means working for themselves. Others work for an electrician who runs a small business and employs a number of other electricians. Some electricians work for specialized companies, such as those that sell and install telecommunications equipment, security systems, or heating, air-conditioning, and ventilation systems. Electricians that work independently, or in electrical businesses, may be hired to work as subcontractors by general contractors constructing residential or commercial buildings.

When working on large industrial projects such as an airport or a large factory complex, electricians must be especially careful. Massive construction projects require vast amounts of material. Some of this material, such as insulation, may be hazardous. In the case of a factory, there may be hazardous chemicals on-site that are used in the production process. Electricians must ascertain what material will be in the area where they are working and take appropriate precautions. Another hazard of large construction projects is equipment. There may be large cranes, possibly moving heavy beams and other material, and large generators producing power for tools and equipment. Electricians need to make sure they are aware of where equipment is and what it is doing.

Specialty Work

Some electricians work in specialty areas. These electricians have skills and knowledge in a particular application beyond those of a general electrician. One area is railway applications. This type of electrician works on diesel or electrical trains whose electrical systems need to be installed and repaired by electricians with expertise in this particular area. In some cases, the electricians may work for a particular rail company, such as Union Pacific. In this case, the electrician is responsible for inspecting, troubleshooting, maintaining, and repairing the electrical components of trains. Diesel electricians also work on the electrical systems of diesel trucks, electric cars, ships, and submarines.

Aviation electricians work on the electrical systems of aircraft, including airplanes and helicopters. Electrical systems in aircraft run the interior and exterior lights, the gauges that provide information to the pilot, the controls he or she uses to fly the plane, the landing gear, the communication system, and almost everything else. Aviation technicians must test, clean, maintain, and repair aircrafts' electrical systems. The largest employer of aviation electricians is the military. However, they are also employed by companies that manufacture aircraft and aircraft systems and by airlines. Another specialty area is government and military facilities. Electricians who work on large industrial and government projects are sometimes employed on projects overseas. These types of jobs require being able to work in a foreign country with people of another culture.

Manufacturing plant electricians are employed by a factory to install, test, maintain, and repair the automated systems used to manufacture products. In addition to the usual electrical knowledge of areas such as wiring, they must understand how to test, install, and repair the electronic components, such as circuit boards, that are used to run machinery. They sometimes repair equipment on the factory floor. At other times, they remove components and work on them in a separate area. When working on a factory floor, they may have to work in noisy and cramped circumstances.

Power plant electricians work for utilities that generate the energy that powers homes and businesses. They regulate the electrical systems that distribute electricity. The electricity is generated by a variety of sources, such as coal- or oil-fired turbines and generators, solar or wind technologies, or a combination of these. Therefore, power plant technicians will need to have knowledge of the technologies that a particular power plant uses. In addition to installing and maintaining the components of the power-generating systems, they must also test and adjust the gauges and devices that control the output of electricity to make sure they are working correctly and that their results are accurate. In addition to electrical training, they must also have training in electronics. Power plant electricians who work in nuclear power plants must undergo additional training and licensing.

The variety of working environments and types of jobs within the electrical industry allows you to choose the nature of the electrical career you want. Do you want to work on large projects in collaboration with a large team, or would you rather work on smaller residential projects with more predictable hours and less stress? Would you prefer to be a general electrician working on a variety of projects, or would you rather have a specialty? The following chapters will provide you with more information that may help you make a decision about your career.

An important part of training to become an electrician is learning to prepare electrical components so they comply with electrical codes.

CHAPTER 2

Becoming an Electrician

Exactly what skills an electrician needs depends on the type of electrical work he or she does. All electricians use math, but the level of required math varies. A residential electrician, who primarily runs household wiring and installs outlets and fixtures, requires less advanced math than one who designs advanced electrical systems for new facilities such as hospitals and factories—but both need to understand the necessary mathematical calculations. All electricians working in the United States must have a thorough knowledge of the National Electrical Code. This is a series of rules and regulations governing every aspect of electrical work, which is maintained by the National Fire Protection Association (NFPA). When a contractor says that an electrical system is "up to code," this means that it meets at least the minimum requirements of the National Electrical Code as well as any state and local codes. Learning about the code is part of all electrician training programs. The code is updated periodically, so even licensed electricians need to check the NFPA website periodically to remain current with the latest regulations.

Electricians have to understand how to perform the tasks demanded by the specific type of electrical work they do. For instance, residential electricians run wire, bend conduit, and calculate how much electrical power and how many circuits are required for a particular home, according to its size. Industrial electricians must be able to install electronic monitoring and control systems. Commercial electricians work with equipment such as industrial heating and air-conditioning systems that are many times larger than those used in the typical home and therefore have different installation requirements.

All electricians begin by learning the basic skills required to be an electrician. This may occur either on the job or in an academic course. However, those interested in pursuing a particular type of electrical work often go on to programs offered by schools or professional associations that teach the specific skills required by that area of work.

Electricians need to be able to think in a logical way and solve problems systematically. For this reason, training programs require students to do hands-on projects that force them to figure out how to meet the requirements of the exercise. You do not need to wait until you are in an electrical training program to learn how to think logically and solve problems, however. Many of your courses in high school require you to use such skills. For example, the papers you write for courses such as English composition and history require you to organize your thoughts in logical order and create sound arguments to support your ideas. Science courses certainly require you to figure out why things act the way they do. Take advantage of these opportunities to hone your logic and problem-solving skills.

Preparing in High School

The time to start preparing for a career as an electrician is while you are in high school. Whether you get a job directly out of high school or go on to further training, you are going to need an academic foundation in areas like math and English. Moreover, if you are looking for a trade that you can begin right out of school, you may want to consider a vocational program while in high school that will give you specific skills.

General Courses

To repair, install, and modify electrical components, you will need to do mathematical equations. Therefore, you need to take math courses in high school, including algebra, precalculus, and geometry. Taking a course in statistics is also helpful. In addition, knowledge of physics is useful for understanding why electricity and electrical components behave the way they do. Today, every field, including the electrical industry, requires computer knowledge, so if your school offers classes in computing, it is beneficial to take them. Also, as an electrician, especially one working on large construction projects, you will need to record information on a computer and write reports, so a class in keyboarding or typing will come in handy—so you don't have to "hunt and peck" to input information.

Verbal and written communication is a vital part of being an electrician, especially if you work on a construction team or have your own business. Therefore, you should take courses in English, especially English grammar and composition. Speaking and writing clearly prevents confusion and misunderstandings, both of which can be costly. It is also a good idea to study another language—one used by a significant number of people in the area in which you live or want to work. Today, people of many different backgrounds work in construction.

Some of your customers will also speak languages other than English. Knowing a second language, such as Spanish, can give you an advantage when you are applying for a job or building up your business. In addition, if you are offered the opportunity to work on a project overseas, knowing a second language may be helpful.

Electrical work can be physically challenging. You may have to climb and maneuver in awkward spaces. You will have to carry heavy tools and components. Therefore, being physically fit will make your job easier. Engage in some type of regular physical activity, whether it is playing on a sports team or performing an independent activity such as swimming, running, or biking. Not only will this activity strengthen your muscles, but it will also get your heart and other organs in shape for doing a physically demanding job. Getting and staying fit are important. A course you might want to take outside of school is a cardiopulmonary resuscitation (CPR) course offered by organizations such as the Red Cross and the American Heart Association. Working as an electrician can put you and the people you work with in dangerous situations. CPR courses provide you with information on lifesaving techniques that you may need in emergency situations.

Vocational and Technical Programs

Some school systems offer vocational programs at the high school level, and some cities have dedicated technical or vocational high schools. Enrolling in this type of program equips students to get a job as soon as they graduate from high school. Upon graduating, students can apply for an apprentice program or a position as a junior-level electrician with an electrical contractor, who can provide more advanced on-the-job training. The curriculum of a typical vocational program in this area covers residential, commercial, and industrial circuitry. It covers electrical theory but also includes shop classes, where students learn practical hands-on techniques. Students study math needed by electricians, how to read and draw electrical diagrams, the rules in their state's electrical code, and basic wiring methods. They learn about devices such as motors, generators, controllers, **transformers**, fire and security alarm circuits, heating systems, and programmable logic controllers (which are used to run automated equipment). How to use test equipment is also covered. Students are taught safety procedures, including the proper use of both hand and power tools. In shop classes, they engage in activities that start with simple projects, such as wiring a light fixture or switch, and advance to more complex projects.

Students will most likely have to complete a series of projects demonstrating their knowledge of increasingly advanced electrical concepts. Students will also have to complete reading, writing, and math assignments. These are designed to be relevant to the electrical field. As with any other high school program, students will have to pass quizzes and tests. Students may also have to write papers on electrical topics and/or successfully complete an independent project—especially in their senior year.

In some vocational programs, junior- and senior-year students have the opportunity to work in cooperative programs—usually called co-ops for short—with local businesses. They might also work on electrical projects at the school or in the community as part of the program.

If your school offers a vocational or technical program in business, see if you can take an accounting class. Many electricians, even those who start out working for someone else, eventually start their own businesses. Most businesses fail not because of lack of technical knowledge but because of poor financial management. A basic knowledge of accounting principles can help you understand and track your finances. Knowing this doesn't hurt when managing your personal finances either. If you are considering working as an independent contractor or running a small business, you might also want to join a

Students in a vocational program gain practical experience while learning how to construct and test electrical components.

program such as Junior Achievement, which encourages students to start a model business. This will give you an understanding of what is involved in running a business.

Further Education

There are a number of ways to acquire training as an electrician. The availability of training programs may be influenced by a variety of local factors. These include the schools offering training, the number of electrical contractors in the area, and the level of construction work being carried out. An area with a lot of construction work and electrical contractors provides more opportunities for on-the-job training. One way to start a career as an electrician is to get a job with an established electrical contractor. The contractor will train you in the practical aspects of doing electrical work on the job. Some larger electrical contracting firms will even pay for employees to attend vocational programs. Others require that junior electricians already have some educational background from a vocational school or online vocational training program.

College Programs

College-level training programs are available from four-year colleges, community colleges, and technical institutes. Two-year associate's degree programs are available at most of these institutions, while colleges and technical institutes also offer four-year bachelor's degree programs. Some schools also offer certificates of training for electricians. These are nondegree programs that provide students with basic apprentice-level training.

Students in electrician programs learn to safely operate hand and power tools, interpret readings from electrical test instruments, solve mathematical problems related to electrical circuits, and locate and interpret sections of the National Electrical Code regulations as they apply to specific electrical installation jobs. They calculate the materials needed for a specific electrical installation and convert measurements between English and metric units. Students are given components, such as motors, that do not work and must troubleshoot and repair them. They read and interpret construction plans and blueprints, which will be necessary in construction work. They splice cable and install commercial and industrial lighting systems, alarm systems, heating and cooling systems, and special equipment. Students learn how to implement the procedures of the Occupational Safety and Health Administration (OSHA) Act, which protect employees in the workplace. Electronics have become an important part of electrical work, so students learn the operational theory and construction of semiconductors, transistors, and other electronic components. They are also taught about telecommunication networks.

Examples of courses taken by electrician students are: Electrical Fundamentals; Installation of Electrical Services; Advanced Calculations for Electricians; High-Voltage Termination and Splicing; Motor Maintenance; Commercial, Industrial, and Specialty Lighting; Fire Alarm Systems; OSHA Standards and Regulations; Introduction to Construction Drawings; Conduit Bending; Electrical Boxes and Fittings; Basic Electronic Theory; Construction Electricity; and Electric Blueprint Reading. Students in degree programs also take a variety of courses

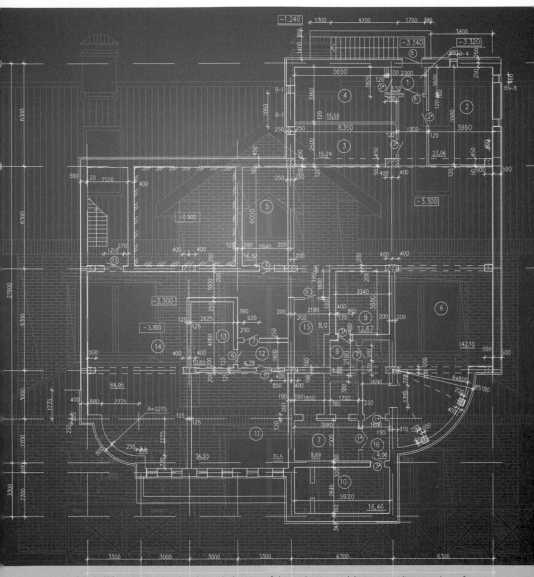

An electrical blueprint is a plan that shows the location of electrical wiring and devices, providing a road map for the electrician.

in other areas such as English composition; business; construction; computer science, such as computer-aided design/computer-aided manufacturing (CAD-CAM) drafting; foreign languages; and humanities.

Some colleges offer co-ops that combine internship or apprenticeship programs with academic training. An internship is usually an unpaid position with a firm in the field. Participating in an internship allows you to experience what life on the job is like. You can see if you like the job and can handle the physical and technical demands. It provides an opportunity to experience how professionals interact with other contractors and customers. It can also give you contacts in the industry who can later provide you with a reference when you are looking for a job.

Another option for higher education in the electrical field is to take an online certificate or degree program. An advantage of an online program is that you can complete the course at home after work while employed. Also, some schools offer payment plans that allow you to make monthly payments. The disadvantage is that you don't get the same level of hands-on experience that you do in physical courses. Electrician programs are available that can be completed in as little as four to six months. These are not degree programs, but they provide a diploma or certificate proving that you have had basic training in the field. When you enroll in an online program, you receive one or more textbooks. You watch and listen to online lectures, and complete exercises, quizzes, and tests, which you submit via e-mail or online applications. Online programs can be used to complete the academic requirements for an electrician's license while you get your hands-on experience as an apprentice.

There are also schools, such as Thomas Edison State College, that offer bachelor's degrees in electrical technology. Students in an online degree program take electrical courses similar to those taught in brick-and-mortar colleges. In addition to more advanced electrical courses than are offered in a certificate program, students in a degree program must also take general courses in areas such as English composition, mathematics, humanities, and science, including physics. If you do decide to enroll in an online program, make sure that the school is accredited. You can look up online colleges by name on the US Department of Education website, which maintains a database of accredited colleges. Making sure the school is accredited ensures that the degree you obtain is valid, and that you can transfer credits you obtain online from a certificate course to another school, if you later decide to pursue a degree in electrical technology or electrical engineering.

Requirements for licensing differ from state to state. You may be required to complete additional hands-on training for licensing in some states. It's important to check your state's licensing requirements before committing to a specific electrician training program.

Apprenticeship

Apprenticeship programs take four to five years. The advantage of apprenticeship programs is that they provide thorough training. Many apprenticeship programs are offered by labor unions and will allow you to become a member of the union. Apprenticeships can also be arranged by working for an electrical contractor or company. Apprentice electricians earn a salary while training, but it is lower than that of fully qualified electricians.

Licensing

In order to practice independently as an electrician, you must have a license. To obtain a license, you must complete your state's requirements for academic and practical training. Although the National Electrical Code sets out the rules and regulations followed by electricians, there is no national licensing process for electricians. Each state has its own licensing requirements and examination. In addition, some cities have their own regulations and licensing requirements. Regardless of jurisdiction, all states recognize three basic levels of electricians:

apprentice, journeyman, and master. Licensing is not the end of an electrician's education.

Because licensing requirements vary from state to state, before starting training to become an electrician, you must check the licensing requirements in your state to make sure you will be able to complete them all. In most cases, in order to obtain a license, you have to be eighteen years old, have a high school diploma or GED (General Educational Development or high school equivalency) certificate, and pass math and English tests.

In most cases, to be granted a license, you must complete a certain number of years practicing under the supervision of a fully licensed electrician and pass a test. Most states have different levels of licenses. A trainee license allows a trainee or apprentice electrician to work under a licensed electrician in order to learn the trade. Trainee licenses are only available to students in an apprenticeship program or working for a master electrician who agrees to supervise them and keep track of their hours worked. Typically, trainee electricians must work 2,000 hours and take at least 144 hours of academic training. Some states allow trainees to get all their training on the job. These states give trainee licenses to individuals who have worked 2,000 hours for an electrical

HELP IN FINDING AN APPRENTICESHIP

There are a number of organizations that provide assistance in finding apprenticeship opportunities. The National Association of Women in Construction is one organization that assists women in entering construction trades. Their website provides information on apprenticeship programs, including those for

On the job, an apprentice electrician is taught how to install and repair electrical systems by a master or journeyman electrician.

apprentice electricians. It also provides information on training programs and scholarship programs for women seeking to learn a construction trade.

Job Corps is a program sponsored by the US Department of Labor. Its goal is to provide career-related education and pre-apprentice training to low-income youth who are at least sixteen years old. It offers a training program in construction, including electrical work. HBI, previously the Manpower Development and Training Department of the National Homebuilders Association, is an organization that offers pre-apprentice certification for disadvantaged and court-involved students, under a grant from the US Department of Justice. It provides construction trade training, job placement assistance, and mentoring to students. Some states offer training grants to women or minorities. For example, the Minnesota Department of Labor provides grants to women who want to enter an apprenticeship program. Check with your state department of labor or employment office to learn what funding may be available to train for a trade. Children of veterans may be eligible for educational assistance under the GI Bill. Contact the Veterans Administration to see if you are eligible.

contractor, and let them get a full electrician's license after 8,000 hours of hands-on work.

A journeyman electrician may be licensed as such in a given jurisdiction, but he or she is still limited to working with a master electrician. Master electricians can work completely independently. To obtain a license, electricians will need to be familiar with the electrical code of the state(s) where they wish to operate. These codes are similar to the National Electrical Code but may vary in specific areas. Even after becoming licensed as a master electrician, you may be required to take continuing education courses at regular intervals, such as once a year, to maintain your license. These courses are offered by professional organizations as well as by colleges and technical schools. They are often available online as well as in person. These continuing education requirements ensure that electricians stay up to date with the latest code regulations and technology.

Advanced/Specialty Licensing

To work in some industries, such as at a nuclear power plant, electricians require additional certification. They must study procedures and processes specific to the industry. This ensures that the electrician is knowledgeable about the particular equipment used in the industry. Equally

These aviation electricians are working together to repair a damaged helicopter engine.

important, it ensures that electricians are familiar with the safety procedures necessary to protect themselves and others.

After Apprenticeship

A journeyman electrician is fully trained. He or she has the experience and training to independently perform tasks assigned by a master electrician. If a journeyman electrician encounters unexpected problems or complications, he or she can discuss these with the master electrician. A master electrician manages projects, or in some cases an electrical company. The master gets permits for construction, designs installations, and oversees the work of journeymen and apprentices. Both journeymen and masters must have work experience, based on years of service or hours of work. Both can take classes in vocational and technical schools, colleges, or programs run jointly by the National Electrical Contractors Association and International Brotherhood of Electrical Workers. There also are several online educational systems. Both are also required to take annual continuing education courses to keep up to date.

Journeyman

A journeyman has several years of experience and has successfully obtained a license. A journeyman can install wiring, fixtures, and other electrical components without supervision. Journeymen are often sent out on service calls of a routine nature. On a construction site, a journeyman performs independent activities according to the plans laid out by the master electrician. One special type of journeyman electrician is a lineman. Linemen work for utilities, telecommunications companies, and cable companies. At utility companies, they work on power lines, generators used for electricity distribution, and telephone and cable lines. At telecommunications and cable companies, they install and service telephone, cable TV, and data transmission lines.

Master Electrician

A person is qualified to become a master electrician after serving three to six years as a journeyman and completing formal education in electricity, project management, and safety regulations and building codes. A journeyman electrician can take the courses necessary to qualify for the master exam at a brick-and-mortar or online school. Many professional organizations in the industry offer such courses as well. To become a master electrician, a person must pass a specific licensing test.

A master electrician designs projects and applies for the necessary permits. Only master electricians can obtain permits for the electrical portion of construction work. The master draws up the plans and makes the decision as to the types of wiring and components used on a project. He or she determines the layout of electrical components. The master supervises journeyman electricians, who perform work according to the plan, and trains apprentices. Once electricians are masters, they can start their own company. Not everyone wishes to take on the burden of running a company, and some master electricians prefer to work for a contractor.

Working as an Electrician

Once you are licensed as a master electrician, you have various options for employment. One option is to work for a contractor or company. In this case, someone else owns the company, and he or she will be responsible for the business aspects of the organization. You will be paid a salary and usually receive benefits such as health insurance and paid vacation. You might work for a company that provides general electrical services, such as XYZ Electrical Services, or a company that requires staff electricians to install the systems it sells. Examples of such companies are those selling HVAC, security, factory automation, or telecommunications systems.

The advantages of working for a company are that you are guaranteed a salary, you usually receive benefits, and you do not have to deal with the responsibilities of running your own business. The disadvantage is that you do not have control over which projects or which types of work you are assigned. A supervisor or scheduler will look at the appointments that need to be addressed and assign electricians. Depending on the company, you may find yourself doing the same type of work repeatedly. Your salary will be a set amount. On one hand, this means that you know how much money you will receive each month, and you are not dependent on finding clients. On the other, the amount you earn is capped.

Working for Yourself

Many electricians choose to work as independent contractors. In this case, they are responsible for finding clients and doing the work themselves. Being an independent contractor gives you the opportunity to apply for projects that interest you. Some electricians do residential work only. They advertise their services, frequently in the telephone book, in local giveaway flyers, and/or through online websites such as HomeAdvisor.com or Angie's List. Others apply for electrician jobs on large construction projects.

Some master electricians start their own companies. In this case, they have business as well as technical responsibilities. Running a business means being able to handle budgeting, accounting, inventory, and human resources responsibilities. If you have your own company, you need at least one clerical employee who answers the phone and handles activities such as ordering supplies. In most cases, you will have other electricians working for you, possibly including journeymen and apprentices. If you have apprentices, you will be responsible for keeping track of their hours worked and ensuring they receive proper training.

If your company handles construction contracting work, you will need to prepare electrical plans, apply for permits for the electrical work, draft electrical construction drawings, and supervise the personnel you send to perform the work. By the time you become a master electrician, you should have the skills required for the technical side of the job. However, you should take some courses in business finance, human resources management, marketing, and accounting to ensure that you have the necessary skills to run a business. Such courses are available from local colleges, including evening and online classes.

When you work for yourself, your earnings are limited only by how much business you bring in. This can be both an advantage and a disadvantage. If you are good at finding customers and projects, you can earn more. However, if times are hard or you are not good at marketing, you may earn less than you would by working for someone else. One advantage of working for yourself is that you are the boss. You decide what projects or jobs to take, and you make all the decisions.

Joining a Union

Labor unions are organizations composed of workers in a particular trade or group of related trades. There are

As an independent contractor, an electrician often has his own van to carry his tools and equipment to different jobsites.

various unions that represent workers in construction trades. When you join a union, you pay monthly dues, which are deducted automatically from your paycheck and sent to the union. In return, the union negotiates with employers on behalf of the members. The result of the negotiations is a collective bargaining agreement. This agreement is a contract that spells out the pay, benefits, and working conditions that apply to the union members.

Union membership confers a number of benefits on members. Union members often receive higher pay and better benefits than individual contractors because the union has a large number of members and therefore more power to negotiate than a single person. Individual contractors can be fired at any time for any reason, but an employer must show due cause (an acceptable reason) before firing a union member. Therefore, membership can provide greater job security. Some unions maintain benevolent funds, which can be used to help members in case of emergency.

Union workers band together to stand up for their rights as workers. Together they have more power than they would have individually.

One of the cons of membership is that if an agreement cannot be reached, the union may call a strike. During a strike, union workers may be without work for an extended period. Union members also sacrifice independence. Even if you disagree with the decisions of the union, you must abide by them. Because unions work on a seniority system, not a merit-based system, advancement opportunities may be limited. When a position needs to be filled, the job goes to the member who's been with the union longest. Therefore, new workers are less likely to find work in hard times, and it may take a long time for them to advance to more desirable jobs.

On the job, an apprentice electrician connects electrical wires to complete an installation.

CHAPTER 3

On the Job

What is it like to be an electrician? What do electricians do on a day-to-day basis? What type of activities and responsibilities can you expect at the different levels of experience?

Working as an Electrical Apprentice

The work an electrician does on a construction project depends on his or her level of expertise. On a construction job, apprentices are primarily there to learn. In the course of a day, they may carry materials and assemble and hang fixtures. Metal tubing or pipes called conduit must be put in place so wires can be run through them. Apprentices help the journeymen who are bending and installing conduit. They may also mount electrical boxes, wire switches, outlets, and phones. Apprentices perform

This photo shows electrical conduit, which are pipes or tubing through which electrical wires are run.

cleanup tasks. After work they attend training classes. For union apprentices, these usually occur three days a week in the early evening after work.

Working as a Journeyman

On a construction project, journeymen work independently on specific applications. They install conduits and run wires; install electrical components, such as switches; and install electronic devices that control security or heating and cooling systems. Although the foreman decides who does what, journeymen are often able to work on the areas they prefer, such as wiring or installing devices.

One of the goals of a journeyman is to earn the respect of his or her fellow electricians. In addition to personal pride, this can have an effect on future employment, or in the case of construction, getting work on future projects.

Respect will be earned by doing excellent work on the job and getting along with other contractors.

After working eight hours or more on a job during the day, journeymen often spend two to three hours in a physical or online class in order to learn additional skills.

Working as a Residential Electrician

An electrician's job starts early in the morning. If an electrician is self-employed, he or she typically checks the answering machine for calls from customers and returns them. The electrician makes new appointments based on what is already scheduled. Visits may be scheduled for the same day if they are emergencies, or for a future date and time if they are for routine work. If there is paperwork to do or materials or equipment to be ordered, based on the previous day's work, the electrician will take care of this. If the electrician works for a company or contractor, there may be office staff that handles the ordering and scheduling. Either way, the electrician reviews the list of appointments and then heads out, usually in a van that contains the tools and components necessary to do electrical work. The residential electrician will do many different types of work, installing new wiring or devices in some locations and determining why the electricity is not working properly at others.

If a room in a home is being renovated, the electrician may need to install new wiring or outlets or switches. The electrician may have to climb through a narrow hatch into an attic and then balance on the ceiling joists. He or she may have to carry wire and tools into the attic and use a flashlight to see. The electrician will then have to position the wire in the attic and possibly cut an opening in the ceiling so that the wire can be put through it to hook up a ceiling fan or fixture. The actual installation of the fixture would require standing on a ladder and hooking it up to the wire. The electrician may be asked to install additional power outlets. This requires cutting an opening in the wall for the new outlet, finding existing wiring, and attaching new wiring from it to the outlet. When he or she is done, the electrician must sweep or vacuum any debris from the work. At another call, the electrician might have to climb a tall ladder to install an exterior safety light near the edge of a roof. After finishing each job, he or she drives back to the office and turns in the copies of the paperwork written on the job, showing the charges and quotes given to customers during the day. This information will be entered into the company's accounting and quote-tracking systems. Leaving the company's van, the electrician takes his or her own car home. After dinner, an electrician might use the computer to access a licensing preparation course over the Internet in order to study for the master electrician's licensing exam.

Another electrician might get a call that someone has no power to the lower part of the house. He or she will have to check the common reasons for this problem. The electrician will ask questions such as, "Has the problem happened before?" He or she will check the breaker box to make sure that the **circuit breakers** to the area haven't snapped open. If one has, this means that the line to that area is overloaded and an additional line needs to be installed. If this is not the case, the electrician looks for other problems. This may mean crawling through a crawlspace under the house to check the wiring, to see if an animal—possibly a mouse—has chewed through the insulation on the line. He or she will have to work in the tight space, using a flashlight to see, to remove old wiring and replace it.

At one time, residential electricians primarily installed outlets, light fixtures, and appliances. The increasing emphasis on technology, energy efficiency, and security has made it necessary for residential electricians to install cable for home computer networks, hardwired smoke detectors and fire alarms that signal the fire station, home security systems, and energy management systems.

Suppose a residential telecommunications electrician is sent to a house where a family has just moved in. They need to have phones installed in various rooms and data lines put in place for computers and for downloading video to the high-definition TVs in the bedrooms and living room. The electrician first locates the phone line that runs to the house. He or she runs cable from the line to the locations where phone jacks are needed, and then installs the phone jacks. He or she runs **fiber-optic** cable from the locations where the TVs will be connected and installs a cable modem, which allows the family's data devices to connect to the phone company's fiber-optic data transmission network. Before leaving, the electrician tests the connected devices to make sure the line works.

Working on Construction Projects

On residential construction jobs, electricians wire single-family and multifamily homes. They may work on a single house or on multiple houses if a contractor is constructing an entire housing development. An electrician may be needed to install appliances in a series of houses being constructed in a new housing development. She will have to install electrical wiring with the appropriate amperage and wattage for the appliances. She will install special types of safety outlets for appliances such as garbage

An electrician runs electrical wires and cables throughout a building under construction.

disposals that operate near water. She will have to carry some of the appliances from the contractor's storage area to the kitchen. The fire safety code in the area where she is working might require that smoke detectors be hardwired directly into the house's electrical system so that homeowners cannot disable them by removing the batteries. She must cut holes in the ceilings and wire the smoke detectors into the system.

On commercial and industrial projects, electricians must install the wiring and devices that bring electricity from the power lines into and throughout office buildings, hospitals, schools, sports stadiums, and other large facilities. In addition to wiring the facility, they may install sophisticated systems for vast arrays of stadium lighting and sound systems, rows of video displays, or stations for computers. They may also install facility-wide fire alarm and security systems. Despite the fact that they are installing wiring and equipment inside a building, they often have to work outside to connect the wiring to outside lines and components. In new construction and open-air stadiums, there may not even be walls, so the electricians may have to work outside in all weather. In multistory buildings, they may have to work on upper stories that are not complete.

Electricians must install the electrical infrastructure for lights, heating and air conditioning, refrigeration, audiovisual systems, data, and security systems. In commercial and industrial buildings, they must install wiring to run industrial equipment.

An electrician may have to drive a long distance to a construction project each day. Depending on the size of the project, work can take place over a few days, weeks, or months. The electrician working on new construction prepares for installation work by reading the blueprints and schematics showing where the wiring and electrical components need to go. Before installing wiring, he or she runs (puts in place) the conduit, which must be cut to the correct length and sometimes bent to fit in the spaces it will run through. After running the conduit, the electrician pulls electrical wire—and, in some facilities, cables for data transmission—through the conduit. The electrician places switches and outlets where they will be located when the walls are finished and connects the wires to the switches and outlets. He or she mounts control panels, fuse boxes, or circuit breaker boxes, and screws or solders the other end of the wires to them, and to transformers, for use by equipment. The electrician then tests the lines, switches, and outlets, using test meters. This work is done while standing, often on scaffolding or ladders, kneeling, and crawling through tight spaces. Finally, the electrician must clean up and stow tools, ladders, and leftover material, before driving home.

When working on new buildings under construction, electricians may be exposed to extreme temperatures because the building is incomplete, and it won't have heat or air conditioning until the electrical work is done. Electrical rough-in work (work done just before the walls are closed up) is done indoors. However, if electricians need to install exterior safety lights, security cameras, or breaker boxes, or have to connect industrial HVAC systems on the roof of an industrial building, they may be exposed to any type of weather.

An electrician installs a fuse box, in which wires are connected to circuit breakers to protect against damage caused by electrical faults.

Construction projects are often very noisy. Roofers, carpenters, and plumbers may all be working at the same time as the electricians. There is likely to be pounding and motor noise from compressors and power saws and other power tools. If ground is being graded or concrete is being poured, there may be heavy equipment moving around the area, with accompanying engine noise. The air could be filled with exhaust from construction vehicles, fumes from paint, and dust from drywall, sanding, or insulation. At times, electricians may need to wear a protective mask to avoid breathing in the dust and fumes.

Extreme weather, job-related material, and equipment are not the only hazards on a job. Electricians may have to deal with indigenous wildlife. Wasps often like to build nests in rafters and under roof eaves. When disturbed, they can fly around the work site. Mice and rats can infest sites and appear when the environment is disturbed.

Working as an Industrial Electrician

In-house and independent industrial electricians perform work at manufacturing plants, mills, mines, foundries, and oil rigs. At industrial plants, electricians inspect the components of the electrical system, such as wires, outlets, fixtures, and industrial equipment. They troubleshoot problems such as power interruptions, short circuits, and devices that fail to work, and repair any nonfunctioning components. To do this, they often must read schematics showing the layout of the equipment's wiring.

Industrial electricians perform routine maintenance on plants' systems, testing them to make sure their components are working to specifications. They test electrical and electronic components to make sure their amperage and voltage are correct. They calibrate monitoring devices to make sure they are correctly measuring what they are supposed to measure.

Increasingly, robotic devices have come to be used to manufacture and inspect goods. The electrician must perform maintenance on these robots and verify that they are properly calibrated and working correctly.

Downtime in a factory, mill, or other industrial facility can delay the delivery of products to customers and cost the company money. The failure of equipment in a power-generating company can affect many people. More than that, however, in some cases failure could endanger workers, or in extreme cases, the surrounding community. Therefore, when equipment has a problem, it must be identified and fixed as quickly as possible.

Industrial plants can't afford to be without electricity. In many cases, they have backup generators to supply power when it goes out. However, these generators often can only supply power for a part of a facility or only for a limited period of time. Therefore, if a plant has a problem that causes the electricity to go out, the electrician must find the problem as quickly as possible and fix it. If the plant does not have an adequate source of backup power, the electrician must find a temporary way to supply power until the problem can be solved.

Because many large facilities run two or three eight-hour shifts—sometimes running twenty-four hours—industrial electricians can be called at any time of the day or night. Since time is of the essence, they have to respond

Modern factories rely on automated equipment run by electrical and electronic devices.

immediately, so they sometimes work outside of normal working hours, such as late at night.

Working as an Outside Lineman

Outside linemen build, maintain, and repair the power lines and components that carry power from the generating source or power plant to the homes and businesses where it is used. They also install and repair streetlights, traffic lights, and train crossing signals. These men and women work primarily outdoors. Being an outside lineman is a physically demanding job. They assemble and put up the metal towers and wooden poles that hold the power lines. Once the physical structure is

ENTERTAINMENT ELECTRICIANS

There are many opportunities to specialize as an electrician. Some electricians work in the entertainment industry. They are called lighting technicians. They may work for movie or TV studios, providing the electrical setup for on-location or studio filming. They are also employed by clubs and concert venues to provide lighting, special effects, and pyrotechnics (fireworks), and in theaters where plays are performed. Lighting technicians must know the special requirements for lighting films and performances. They set up and run lights and special effects during productions. They often have to work on catwalks high above the floor of a stage.

The head of a studio electrical department is called the "gaffer." He or she designs the lighting plans for productions. Because filming and performances can take place at any hour, a lighting technician's working hours are dictated by the type and timing of the performance or production he or she is providing lighting for. Jobs as lighting technicians can be located by checking for ads on online jobsites and in industry publications, or by contacting the human resources department of performance venues directly.

Some lighting technicians begin by qualifying as general electricians and then learn the particular requirements of lighting on the job. However, many take special courses in lighting and/or special effects for film or theater.

An electrical lineman works high above the ground to repair a faulty component on a high-voltage power line.

erected, they install hardware, **conductors**, transformers, and other electrical components. Outside linemen spend much of their time high in the air. They climb utility poles on a regular basis and develop strong climbing skills. In areas where electrical or fiber-optic cables run underground, outside linemen install the underground cables and electrical components. They must attach and repair lines that can carry as much as 500,000 volts of electricity. Outside linemen often have to work in bad weather. Storms tend to damage the electrical components and lines strung from poles and towers, resulting in loss of power, often to a significant area. Repairing the electrical transmission system is critical. Therefore, it is often necessary to perform work in stormy conditions or in the difficult conditions immediately following a bad storm. This work is very dangerous. Contact with the wires or components carrying live electricity can result in serious injury or even death.

Working as a Commercial Telecommunications Technician

One area that has grown tremendously in importance, from the latter half of the twentieth century to the present, is telecommunications. Telecommunications is the transmission of signals electronically over wires. At one time, telecommunications relied on copper wires bundled into cables. Today, much of telecommunications uses fiber-optic cables, which are composed of thin strands, or fibers, of glass.

Telecommunications technicians are electricians who install the wiring and components for voice, data, and video transmission. Telecommunications technicians install low-voltage lines and components, as opposed to the high-voltage lines and devices that outside linemen work with. The components that control the distribution of voice and data around a facility are housed in one place, called the telecommunications room or closet. The technician installs control devices and equipment, including telephone switches and hubs for computer networks, among other devices. The technician then must run cables for telephone, data, and video transmission throughout the facility and connect them to the control devices in the telecommunications room. In new construction, the cabling can be done before the walls go up. Often, however, telecommunications technicians must run cable and install devices in existing buildings, some of which are many years old, which can be a challenge. Telecommunications technicians work primarily indoors. Often they must work in tight spaces. They must lift devices such as file servers and telecommunications hubs.

Working as an Electrical Foreman

If an electrician gains enough knowledge and experience, he or she may become an electrical foreman. The foreman is the boss of a team of electricians. An electrical foreman can be a journeyman or a master electrician. The foreman puts a crew of electricians together and supervises their work on a construction project. Many large construction projects use union labor. In a union project, the foreman of the project gets the electricians for the project through the union hiring hall, which is a union employment office. Employers notify the union about upcoming projects for which they need workers. When an electrician is available for work, he or she signs up on a list. Qualified people are assigned to a project in the order in which they signed the list. Because of the union rules for assigning members to jobs, foremen cannot just hire people they know from previous jobs. Therefore, a foreman must be skilled at making a team work. Although there are rules for how workers are assigned to jobs, the workers are not required to accept a job, so a foreman must rely on his or her good reputation to attract the best workers. If an electrician is a foreman on a nonunion project, he or she is free to hire anyone. In this case, the foreman may hire people he or she knows or has worked with on previous projects.

All foremen must display qualities of fairness, knowledge, and the ability to ensure that their teams have the necessary tools, material, and information. Foremen must be skilled in getting good work out of their people without being a bully or an autocrat. Otherwise, other electricians will not be willing to work for them in the future.

Managing a team of electricians is much like managing employees in any enterprise. One has to lead by example, demonstrating knowledge and skill. The foreman has to assign work fairly. He or she needs to address any issues or problems team members have. Sometimes it is necessary to correct a team member. If this is done in a fair manner, then the other team members will believe that the foreman is fair. The ability to put together a good team and get them to work well together makes a foreman successful.

The Dangers of the Job

The first thing that comes to mind when people think of the dangers of electrical work is getting shocked. Electricians do have to be careful and know how to properly ground themselves, but since most electricians work with low voltage, getting a shock is rarely fatal. The exception is linemen who work with high-voltage lines. They must take special precautions and be certain they do not come into contact with the lines because contact can cause serious, even fatal, injuries. Your body conducts electricity. Shocks occur when you touch an object that conducts electricity (such as a metal panel in contact with a live wire), and electricity flows from that object through you into the ground or into an object in contact with the ground, such as a pipe. The same thing will occur if you are touching the metal part of a tool that comes in contact with a wire or other conductor. The most important effect that low-voltage shocks cause is—well, shock. Being shocked can cause a person to recoil or jump back. If you are on a ladder or standing on a ceiling joist, this can result in a dangerous fall.

Protecting themselves from shocks requires electricians to be insulated. Being insulated means the electricity cannot pass through you into the ground. The most common type of insulation is rubber-soled shoes because rubber doesn't conduct electricity. For the same reason, standing on wood rather than the ground provides insulation. You need to avoid standing on wet surfaces when working because water is a conductor. For the same reason, keeping your hands dry when working is a good idea.

There are many other ways in which electricians can be injured on the job. Electricians can hurt themselves when working with tools. They might cut themselves when stripping wire or catch a hand on a protruding nail. Falls are common; electricians work on roofs and ladders, and in attics where they can slip on planks and break through the drywall covering a ceiling. They can pull muscles and injure their backs when lifting heavy ladders, equipment, or appliances. To protect yourself on the job, it is important to know the proper way to approach each situation. This can be as simple as always stripping wire away from your hand and tying back long hair so it doesn't get caught in equipment. It is also important to pay attention to your surroundings. Examine the environment where you will be working. Know where it is safe to place your feet, for example.

Pros and Cons of an Electrical Career

The advantages of being an electrician include having a constant variety of new activities to do and different problems to solve. Because the field constantly changes as new types of electrical technologies and devices are developed, it stays interesting, and there are always new things to learn. Having solid training and experience as an electrician provides you with the option of specializing in a wide variety of industries that employ electricians. In addition, the salaries or hourly pay rates of fully qualified electricians are quite good.

One of the disadvantages of a career as an electrician is that it can be dangerous. Electrical objects used on the job can injure the electrician or other people. Therefore, this is a job for someone who is cautious, patient, and detail-oriented. New technologies, devices, and equipment are constantly being developed and existing equipment is constantly evolving as new and improved versions replace older ones. This means that you must make a commitment to constantly update your skills and knowledge by taking online courses and workshops offered by educational or industry organizations.

The need for new housing has created an increasing demand for electricians to work on residential construction projects.

CHAPTER 4

Your Place in the Industry: Present and Future

The National Electrical Contractors Association (NECA) states that the electrical contracting industry does $130 billion in business annually. The NECA estimates that there are approximately 70,000 electrical contracting firms, employing about 650,000 electricians. About two-thirds of electricians work in construction-related jobs. According to the US Department of Labor *Career Outlook Handbook*, jobs for electricians are expected to grow about 20 percent annually through 2022. This is faster than the growth rate for many other jobs. Because more and more electronic devices are being incorporated into new homes and commercial construction, there is likely to be steady demand for electricians in the future. The increase in robotics and automated manufacturing systems is likely to create a continuing demand for industrial electricians. Jobs in the construction industry are dependent on the state of the economy. In the years following the economic crisis of 2008, it was difficult to get financing for a new home. This resulted in a shortage of new houses. If the economy continues to improve, opportunities in the construction industry are likely to increase. Utilities are moving away from coal as the fuel used to generate electricity and toward incorporating alternative energy systems such as solar and wind. As electricity-generating plants expand and upgrade, this will also increase the demand for electricians in the industry.

The median salary for electricians is around $50,000, or about $25 per hour. However, pay varies widely, depending on the level of the electrician. Apprentice electricians generally earn 30 to 50 percent of what experienced electricians earn. Pay is also influenced by the nature of employment: industrial, residential, construction, telecommunications, or special applications. Typically apprentice residential electricians earn $20 to $40 per hour. Pay for apprentice commercial electricians starts around $30 or $40 per hour, and the pay for apprentice industrial electricians starts around $40 to $50. The rate of pay will increase as electricians move to the journeyman level.

Electricians in specialty areas, such as nuclear power generation, and outside line workers earn higher salaries because of the greater risk of injury and greater expertise required for the job. The pay rates of union electricians are often higher than those of nonunion electricians, but they must pay monthly union dues from their salary, which reduces their take-home pay. The amount of money that self-employed electricians can earn is limited only by how many customers they can serve and how efficiently they run their company.

The pay for electricians who are willing to work on projects overseas, such as energy infrastructure projects, is often even higher. They can earn as much as $75 to $100 per hour. However, given the political unrest and attitudes toward Americans in some parts of the world, such work could involve personal safety risks.

Like the general population, the pool of electricians is aging. Many people born during the baby boom of the 1950s and 1960s are retiring. As older electricians retire, this creates a need for new apprentices to enter the trade and for journeymen to move up to positions vacated by retiring master electricians. The shortage of new housing caused by the economic crash of 2008 is now creating a need for new buildings to house the next generation that is starting families. Rents have been rising steadily as more people have rented rather than purchased homes since 2008. Rising rents are likely to fuel a greater interest in purchasing a home, which is likely to fuel an increase in housing construction, as well as a continuing interest in constructing apartment buildings.

As the economy continues to pick up, construction of new commercial and industrial facilities is also likely to increase. All of this bodes well for the employment of electricians. For the 80 percent of electricians who work in the residential industry, it makes little difference whether people own or rent their homes or apartments. Electrical work still needs to be done.

Benefits

The benefits provided to electricians depend on the size of the company they work for. Small businesses may offer health insurance and usually provide paid vacation. Large companies typically offer a variety of benefits for employees, such as health, life, disability, and dental insurance, as well as 401(k) plans, which encourage employees to save for retirement. Some companies offer a tuition reimbursement program. This type of program repays employees for the cost of educational courses they take that increase their job skills. Benefits for union workers are negotiated by the union. Independent contractors are responsible for obtaining their own insurance, and health and disability insurance are definitely recommended.

Finding Work

How you find a job in the electrical field depends on the type of electrician you wish to be, and on the environment in which you wish to work. Do you want to work for a company or independently? If you are a residential electrician or work for a company, you will have work all year long. Homeowners move and have electrical problems at all times of the year. If you work on the construction of new buildings, you will find there is more work at certain times of the year, usually when the weather is favorable. During the winter in northern areas, renovations may go on, but there will probably be fewer jobs overall. To maximize your chances of getting work when jobs are scarce, you need to develop relationships with other electricians and general contractors. The best way to develop a good working relationship is to make a good impression. Show up on time, do good work, and get along with others working on the job. Whenever you have the opportunity to work with other electricians and contractors, exchange business cards. Attend meetings of professional organizations, network with others in the industry, and get their cards. When you have work or need work, you will have people to contact.

You also need to decide whether you wish to be a union or nonunion electrician. If you are interested in becoming a union electrical worker, you should contact the International Brotherhood of Electrical Workers (IBEW). Construction activity is usually slow over the winter and starts to increase in the spring. Therefore, the IBEW typically accepts new apprentices in the spring.

If you prefer nonunion work, you can apply for work at any nonunion electrical contracting company. You can contact companies in your area or use an online job-hunting site to locate companies that have openings. Type "electrician apprentice" into the search tool and you will get a variety of postings for electrical apprentices. The websites of electrical trade organizations have job listings as well. Most companies today list open jobs on their websites. If you are interested in working at a utility, industrial, telecommunications, or similar type of company, check out their sites and look for a "Jobs" or "Careers" page to find openings.

If there is a job fair held in your community, this will provide the opportunity to talk to representatives of companies who are looking to hire. Even if they are not explicitly looking for electricians, the representatives can provide you with information on whom to contact at the company about a job in that area. There is a surprisingly wide range of companies looking to hire electricians, including theme parks, energy exploration firms, and transportation companies.

The administrators of vocational schools often have relationships with businesses in the area and may be able to assist students and graduates in finding work. Most community colleges and technical schools have a placement office whose function is to help students find jobs. Some online schools also provide job-hunting resources or placement assistance.

The best way to find work is by networking with others in the industry. Contacting the people you have worked with while in school or on a project can often provide you with job leads. Participating in professional organizations is a good way to meet other electricians. Join a student chapter of an organization such as the National Homebuilders Association or the Institute of Electrical and Electronic Engineers (IEEE). These chapters give you a chance to develop relationships with other young people interested in the field. Working with a professional organization allows you to learn about the trade and meet professionals who can provide you with advice. Keep the contact information of everyone you meet. When you are ready to look for an apprentice position, contact them and ask if they know of any openings. Even if the person you talk to can't offer you work, he or she may know of someone else who has an opening.

You can contact potential employers by phone or by sending them a cover letter expressing your interest in a job, along with a résumé. Tell potential employers that you are interested in residential work as a first-year apprentice.

The choice of whether or not to join a union may be influenced by where you live or wish to work. Some areas are heavily unionized, especially large cities, and it may be difficult to find nonunion work there. Other, more sparsely populated areas may have few union opportunities. Some cities and states have "right-to-work" laws. These laws prohibit employers from discriminating against nonunion workers when hiring.

Preparing a Résumé

Some places where you apply for work may have an application form. For other companies, you will need to have a résumé. This is a document you give or send to potential employers to show them why you are a good candidate for a job. Your résumé should show any specific education and experience you have that is relevant to the job. However, you also want to emphasize any qualities you have that will make you a good electrician, such as reliability and problem-solving skills.

Since you are looking for an entry-level job, use a simple format, which makes it easy for a potential employer to see if you have the basic qualities to be a good apprentice. Make sure your name, phone number(s), and e-mail address are at the top of the page. State that you are applying for an electrical apprentice position; if you are responding to an ad, specify that job.

Next, list any paid or unpaid jobs you've had. Include part-time, summer, internship, and co-op work you've done. Even if you haven't done electrical work, you can still state that you solved particular problems on the job. Many people who become electricians have a relative in the trade. If you've assisted with electrical projects or acted as an unpaid (or paid) electrician's helper, include this information.

Next, list your educational background. If you've taken a vocational course, state that. If you've taken a standard academic program, list any classes you've taken that apply, such as physics, algebra, geometry, precalculus, and computer science. Finally, include any relevant personal information such as the fact that you build remote-controlled drones as a hobby or speak a language other than English.

It is very important that your résumé be neat and professional looking. Electricians need to be careful and pay attention to detail, so be sure you proofread your résumé and find any typos or errors. Have someone else read it as well. Don't think you can just use a spell checker. It won't spot missing words, and it won't pick up the fact that you've used the wrong word if it's spelled correctly (for example, typing "their" when you mean "there"). An employer is likely to think that if you can't be bothered to check your work on paper, you can't be trusted to do so on the job.

Interviewing for a Job

If an employer thinks you are a good candidate for a job, you will be invited to come in for an interview. This is a chance for the employer to meet you face to face. It is up to you to convince the person interviewing you that you are the best person for the job.

This means you need to look, talk, and behave like a professional. Even though you may be wearing work clothes on the job, go to the interview dressed in neat, clean professional-looking clothing. Your goal is to look neat and tidy—sloppiness is the last thing an employer wants in an electrician. Use proper grammar when you speak and avoid slang. How well you communicate with the person interviewing you is an example of how you will talk to customers. For the same reason, be sure to treat everyone you meet with respect and politeness.

If you are applying at a company or utility, use the Internet to look up information on the company before you go. The interviewer will appreciate the fact that you took the time to do so. Also, having this information will allow you to prepare an explanation in advance of why you would be a good choice for the company. At an interview, you are likely to be asked two types of questions. First, you will be asked job-related questions. Since you are applying for an apprentice position, you will not be expected to have a deep knowledge of the electrical trade. The interviewer will ask questions designed to see if you have the manual and problem-solving skills that will allow you to learn the job. For example, he or she may ask how you would solve a particular problem. The goal of this question is to see how you would go about finding an answer, not to see if you can come up with a solution. (However, if you have completed a vocational program, the employer may ask you basic technical questions to test your knowledge of the aspects of electrical work you are supposed to have mastered.) Second, you will be asked general questions designed to find out how well you work with others, how you handle pressure, and whether you're

PROFESSIONAL ORGANIZATIONS

Professional organizations are an invaluable resource for learning about the industry, accessing training, and meeting professionals who can provide you with information and advice. Some trade organizations offer special resources for students in school or those embarking on a career. Other groups provide support for minority electricians and women in the industry. Participating in trade organizations can help you when you are starting out. Once you are established, they can help you stay up to date with developments in the field and advance in your career. The following is a selection of trade organizations of interest to electricians:

- Association of Edison Illuminating Companies (AEIC): One of the oldest organizations in the electric energy industry, AEIC encourages research and the exchange of technical information. It provides publications on technical topics in the electrical energy industry.

- Association of Energy Engineers (AEE): This is an organization for professionals in the energy management, power generation, energy services, renewable energy, and related industries. It provides training, certification, and job information for members.

- Association of Energy Services Professionals (AESP): AESP provides a range of training courses for electrical and renewable energy professionals.

- Coalition of Labor Union Women (CLUW): America's only national organization for union women. CLUW's mission is to unify all union women to determine and address common problems and concerns.
- Independent Electrical Contractors Association (IECA): A professional association for independent (nonunion) electrical contractors, IECA offers apprenticeship programs at fifty locations around the country, among other activities.
- International Brotherhood of Electrical Workers (IBEW): The IBEW is the union to which electricians belong. It provides training and job information on its website.
- Institute of Electrical and Electronic Engineers (IEEE): The largest organization for professionals working in the electric and electronic industries, the IEEE develops standards, hosts meetings on industry topics, and produces electrical publications. It has a dedicated student website and provides job and internship information.
- National Association of Minority Contractors (NAMC): NAMC provides access, advocacy, and development for members and has chapters around the country.
- National Electrical Contractors Association (NECA): A professional organization for all types of electrical contractors, whose history dates back to 1901, this organization develops standards and connects members with leading companies in the industry. It has 119 chapters around the country.
- National Fire Protection Association (NFPA): The NFPA maintains the National Electrical Code and provides training on it.

reliable and hardworking. Because you are young, the employer may be concerned about whether you will show up on time or whether you will goof off on the job. Be prepared to give concrete examples that show you have the right qualities.

Moving Forward

There are a number of higher-level career paths open to electricians. Many master electricians eventually open their own businesses. Those who take this route concentrate on building up the business, by increasing its size, the number of customers it serves, and the size of the projects it undertakes. There are, however, a number of other options open to master electricians.

If you are a union electrician, you have the option to work your way up to a union management position, first at the local level and potentially at the national level. When you become a manager, you no longer perform the daily tasks of electrical work. Instead, you are involved in the administrative side of running the union itself. You may be involved in organizing unions in nonunionized companies, negotiating with employers and government representatives, and performing the day-to-day tasks involved in running the union.

A master electrician plans the electrical portion of a construction project and supervises the workers on the jobsite.

If you are a full-time employee of a utility, telecommunications company, or industrial plant, you can also work your way into management, eventually becoming head of the electrical or maintenance department. When you become a manager, you are responsible for hiring, firing, scheduling, and supervising workers. You also become responsible for ensuring that the department has adequate equipment and materials while staying within its budget. You may need to make reports to higher-level management regarding the state of equipment and the requirements for upgrades, and obtain approval for necessary expenditures. Again, you will be involved primarily at the supervisory level.

An estimator is an electrician who works for a contractor, calculating the time and cost of materials needed to accomplish a project. Estimators prepare bid proposals. They review project plans to make sure that the labor, time, and supply estimates are accurate. Their job is to make sure that the projects their companies work on are profitable. They play a very important role in large construction projects.

An electrical inspector works for the city. He or she inspects the work performed by contractors on new construction and renovations. The inspector can approve the work or require changes. The inspector's job is to ensure that work is done according to the electrical codes so that the final construction is safe for the building's occupants.

If you find you are interested in designing electrical installations or inventing new devices, an option is to undertake additional education to become an electrical engineer. In contrast to an electrician, who installs, tests, and repairs electrical wiring and equipment, an electrical engineer designs electrical and electronic installations, industrial and consumer devices, equipment, control systems, robots, and other products. Electrical engineers

An electrical inspector checks and tests finished electrical work to ensure it complies with electrical codes.

work in offices, electronics research labs, and industrial plants. They may work in private industry or government facilities. Electrical engineers have at least a bachelor's degree in electrical engineering, and many go on to earn a master's degree or a PhD.

What the Future Holds

The construction industry is moving toward smart buildings. All systems in homes may be connected by computer technology to devices such as cell phones and tablet computers that allow them to be controlled remotely. For example, this technology allows homeowners to turn lights on and off, change thermostat settings, reset alarms, and control appliances from their cell phones.

In many factories, manufacturing has become increasingly automated, and this trend is likely to continue in the future. Many new factories (and older factories that are being upgraded) are installing entire manufacturing lines that are run and monitored solely by computers. Factories will also have an **integrated** electrical system that uses sensors to send information to a computer to issue a warning if there is a problem with any of the factory's systems, such as security, lighting, HVAC, or the manufacturing equipment. Many new apartment and office buildings are being constructed with similar types of integrated electrical control systems. So, whether you work on new construction or fix systems in finished buildings, you will need to be familiar with how computers and computer-controlled systems operate, and how to interact with them when installing and repairing electrical components in buildings.

There is a trend toward installing **photovoltaic** panels in homes and businesses. Photovoltaic panels collect solar

An electrician installs photovoltaic panels, which capture sunlight and convert it into electrical energy.

energy and convert it to electricity, which can travel down an electric line into the home or business. Once installed, the panels save owners the cost of buying electricity from the local power company, which has become very expensive. Electricians will need to become familiar with how to install and troubleshoot building-based photovoltaic systems.

The Greening of Electricity

The need to reduce energy usage is going to continue to be a major influence in the electrical industry. The use of electric cars is likely to continue to increase. This creates a need for electric charging stations. Since there are not many of these available today, electricians will need to install and maintain a significant number of them in the years to come.

Sustainable building has become important in the 2000s, and its importance is likely to continue to grow. Sustainable building means constructing buildings that have as little effect on the environment as possible. **Green building**, among other things, refers to making buildings as energy efficient as possible, by reducing the amount of energy used in lighting, heating, cooling, and ventilating them. It also requires monitoring energy usage so that, for example, temperatures can be adjusted automatically at various times of the day to avoid wasting energy. The demands of green building mean using energy-efficient equipment and incorporating renewable energy technology into new construction. There will also be more demand for retrofitting older homes, businesses, and factories with more energy-efficient electrical equipment. Electricians will need to be familiar with installing, maintaining, and repairing the devices and wiring associated with such systems.

Teamwork is essential on all construction projects. It is important for electricians and other contractors to work together to ensure each job is completed safely, on time, and within budget.

Because of the rising costs of energy to both residential and commercial consumers, there is likely to be a demand for energy management consultants. These consultants evaluate the existing electrical systems in buildings and advise owners on how to upgrade their systems so that they use energy more efficiently, in order to reduce the amount paid for electricity.

The Changing Construction Industry

New computer-based technologies are not only changing what's in buildings—they're also changing how contractors build them. Three-dimensional (3-D) computer technologies are allowing architects and contractors to draw buildings in three dimensions rather than two. As 3-D and virtual reality technology improve, it's likely that instead of just looking at blueprints of a building to see where systems and components are located, the electrician will be able to view those locations in 3-D, virtually "walking around" and examining where these elements will be installed in a building when it is constructed.

Not only are systems in buildings becoming more complex, but they are also becoming more interrelated. For example, heating and cooling systems have traditionally been the realm of plumbers, but now that

Advanced architectural modeling software allows contractors to view buildings in three dimensions.

these systems must be connected to electronic controls for building-wide monitoring and operation, the roles of plumbers and electricians overlap more than in the past. Therefore, the future is likely to see growth in the use of **multidisciplinary** teams when contractors are preparing proposals and quotations for new construction and major renovation projects. In the past, it was common for a general contractor to collect quotes from individual subcontractors, such as plumbers and electricians, and then combine the quotes in a bid proposal. However, in the future, there may be a more collaborative method for preparing proposals, whereby representatives of the various trades work together to arrive at the requirements and costs. There will also be more collaborative work on the project itself. As you can see, the electrical industry is continually evolving, and as an electrician, you will need to keep adapting as well.

Glossary

alternating current An electrical current that moves first in one direction and then reverses and moves back in the other direction along a wire.

circuit An electrical configuration that allows electricity to move from a source to a device and back to the source in a circle.

circuit breaker A device that opens a space in a circuit to stop electricity from traveling around it.

conductor A device through which electricity can flow.

conduit A metal pipe or tube through which wires run.

contractor A person hired to work on a construction project.

fiber-optic Used to describe an object made of glass or plastic that conducts light rather than electricity.

general contractor The head contractor on a job. He or she usually hires the other contractors.

green building A construction approach that minimizes a structure's effect on the environment.

hardwired Being wired directly into the electrical system rather than being plugged into an outlet or battery-operated.

infrastructure The basic systems serving a facility, city, or other area.

insulated Covered in material that prevents electricity from passing through.

integrated Connected to form one centrally controlled system.

multidisciplinary Involving different specialties.

photovoltaics A technology that converts sunlight to electricity.

subcontractor A contractor in a specialty such as electricity or plumbing hired by a general contractor.

sustainable building A construction approach that minimizes a building's effect on the environment; for example, by using energy-efficient materials and equipment, and renewable materials.

transformer A device that changes the voltage and current from one level to another; for example, converting electricity from a high-voltage power line to a level that is safe for home use.

voltage A measure of the force of electricity going through a circuit.

Further Information

Books

Harmon, Daniel E. *Essential Careers: A Career as an Electrician.* New York: Rosen Publishing, 2010.

Hermes, David. *The Electrician's Trade Demystified.* New York: McGraw-Hill, 2013.

Teitelbaum, Michael. *Cool Careers: Electrician.* North Mankato, MN: Cherry Lake Publishing, 2010.

Websites

Explore the Trades
www.explorethetrades.org
This organization's website allows students to explore various aspects of a career in a trade, including being an electrician.

National Joint Apprenticeship Training Committee
Inside Electricians Apprenticeship IBEW
www.youtube.com/watch?v=SwhJi3iMPzs
The NJATC is a collaboration between the National Electrical Contractors Association and the International Brotherhood of Electrical Workers. This video shows what the union apprenticeship program consists of and describes the application procedure and requirements.

Bibliography

Association for Union Democracy. "Hiring Hall Procedures in the Construction Trades," www.uniondemocracy.org/ UDR/132-Hiring_Hall_Procedures_in_the_Construction_ Trades.htm.

Berwick Electric Co. "A Day in the Life of an Electrician: Mike Lucas," www.berwickelectric.com/the-electrical-blog/ bid/68001/A-Day-in-the-Life-of-an-Electrician-Michael-Lucas.

ChooseConstruction.org. "Electricians," chooseconstruction. org/trade_elec.htm#Outside.

Chron. "Differences between a Journey and Master Electrician, work.chron.com/differences-between-journeyman-master-electrician-2158.html.

———. "Clever Ways to Answer Questions in a Job Interview," work.chron.com/clever-ways-answer-questions-job-interview-26744.html.

———. "Job Fair Questions Students Need to Be Prepared to Answer," work.chron.com/job-fair-questions-students-need-prepared-answer-11037.html.

Clever Job Hunter. *Career Guide: How to Become an Electrician.* Amazon Digital Services, 2011.

ECA. "2021: The Future of the Electrical Contracting Industry," www.eca.co.uk/_assets/files/2021-Vision-PDF(1).pdf.

Hermes, David. *The Electrician's Trade Demystified.* New York, McGraw-Hill, 2013.

Inside Jobs. "Aviation electrician." www.insidejobs.com/careers/aviation-electrician.

Institute of Energy Research. "History of Electricity," instituteforenergyresearch.org/history-electricity.

Maricopa Community College. "Construction Trades: Electricity," aztransmac2.asu.edu/cgi-bin/WebObjects/acres.woa/wa/freeForm?id=60447.

National Electrical Contractors Association, www.necanet.org/professional-development/continuing-education-training/specialized-training.

Our Life at Work. "Journeyman Electrician: John Brining," ourlifeatwork.com/?p=41

StateUniversity.com. "Construction Electrician Job Description." Retrieved June 18, 2015. careers.stateuniversity.com/pages/243/Construction-Electrician.html.

Study.com. "What Is a Plant Electrician?" study.com/articles/What_is_a_Plant_Electrician.html.

Thirty-Two Volts. "Want to Be a Lighting Technician?" Retrieved June 18, 2015. www.twothirtyvolts.org.uk/careers/jobs/lighting-technician.html.

Union Pacific. "Diesel Electrician," up.jobs/diesel-electrician.html.

US Department of Labor. "Electricians." In *Occupational Outlook Handbook*, 2012. Retrieved June 19, 2015. www.bls.gov/ooh/construction-and-extraction/electricians.htm.

Index

Page numbers in **boldface** are illustrations. Entries in **boldface** are glossary terms.

About the Author

Jeri Freedman has a bachelor's of arts from Harvard University. For fifteen years she worked for high-technology companies involved in cutting-edge technologies, including advanced semiconductors and scientific testing equipment. She is the author of more than forty young adult nonfiction books, including a number of career guides, such as *Software Development* (High-Tech Jobs series), *Careers in Human Resources*, *Careers in Security*, *Careers in Child Care*, and *Jump-Starting a Career in Hospitals and Home Health Care*, among others.